JAMES BOND 007™
COLLECTION

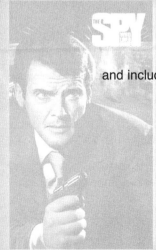

This instrumental series is arranged for Violin, Viola, and Cello and includes a fully orchestrated accompaniment CD. The arrangements are completely compatible with each other and can be played together or as solos.

Project Manager: CAROL CUELLAR
Music Editor: BILL GALLIFORD
Arranged by BILL GALLIFORD, ETHAN NEUBURG and TOD EDMONDSON
Art Layout: MICHAEL RAMSAY
Recordings by ARTEMIS MUSIC LIMITED

CONTENTS

DIAMONDS ARE FOREVER

Lyric by DON BLACK
Music by JOHN BARRY

Diamonds Are Forever - 3 - 1
IFM0403CD

FOR YOUR EYES ONLY

Lyrics by MICHAEL LEESON
Music by BILL CONTI

For Your Eyes Only - 2 - 1
IFM0403CD

FROM RUSSIA WITH LOVE

Words and Music by
LIONEL BART

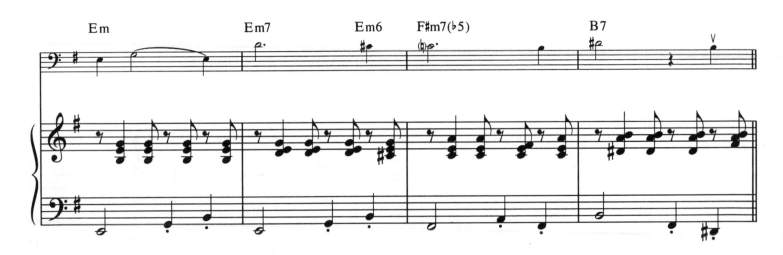

From Russia With Love - 4 - 1
IFM0403CD

10

From Russia With Love - 4 - 3
IFM0403CD

GOLDFINGER

Music by
JOHN BARRY
Lyrics by
LESLIE BRICUSSE
and ANTHONY NEWLEY

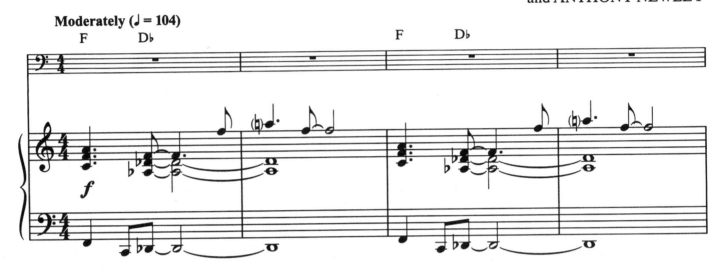

Goldfinger - 4 - 1
IFM0403CD

ON HER MAJESTY'S SECRET SERVICE

Music by JOHN BARRY

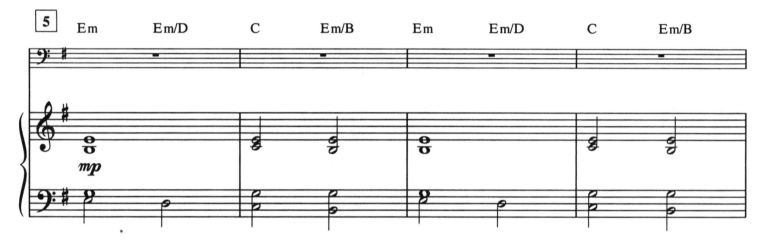

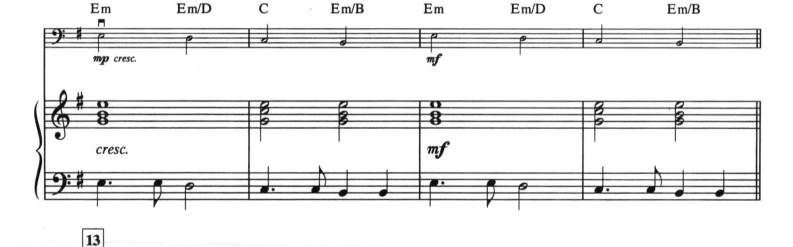

On Her Majesty's Secret Service - 4 - 1
IFM0403CD

JAMES BOND THEME

Music by MONTY NORMAN

James Bond Theme - 4 - 1
IFM0403CD

THUNDERBALL

Lyric by DON BLACK
Music by JOHN BARRY

Thunderball - 4 - 1
IFM0403CD

Thunderball - 4 - 2
IFM0403CD

JAMES BOND 007™
COLLECTION

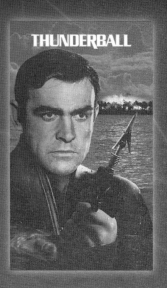

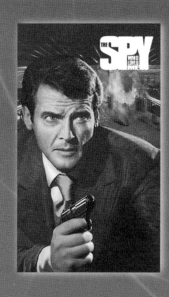

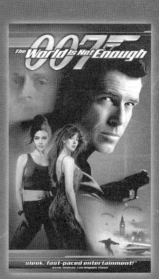

JAMES BOND 007™
COLLECTION

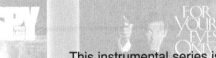

This instrumental series is arranged for Violin, Viola, and Cello and includes a fully orchestrated accompaniment CD. The arrangements are completely compatible with each other and can be played together or as solos.

Project Manager: CAROL CUELLAR
Music Editor: BILL GALLIFORD
Arranged by BILL GALLIFORD, ETHAN NEUBURG and TOD EDMONDSON
Art Layout: MICHAEL RAMSAY
Recordings by ARTEMIS MUSIC LIMITED

CONTENTS

DIAMONDS ARE FOREVER

Lyric by DON BLACK
Music by JOHN BARRY

IFM0403CD

FOR YOUR EYES ONLY

Lyrics by MICHAEL LEESON
Music by BILL CONTI

FROM RUSSIA WITH LOVE

Words and Music by
LIONEL BART

Moderately (♩ = 88)

IFM0403CD

GOLDFINGER

Music by
JOHN BARRY
Lyrics by
LESLIE BRICUSSE
and ANTHONY NEWLEY

Moderately (♩ = 104)

IFM0403CD

ON HER MAJESTY'S SECRET SERVICE

Music by JOHN BARRY

IFM0403CD

JAMES BOND THEME

Music by MONTY NORMAN

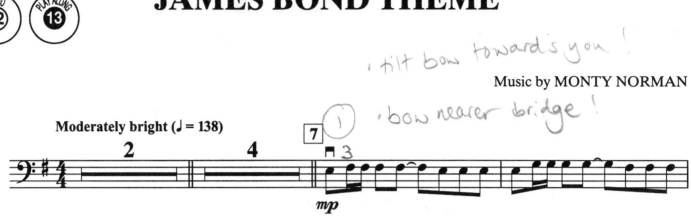

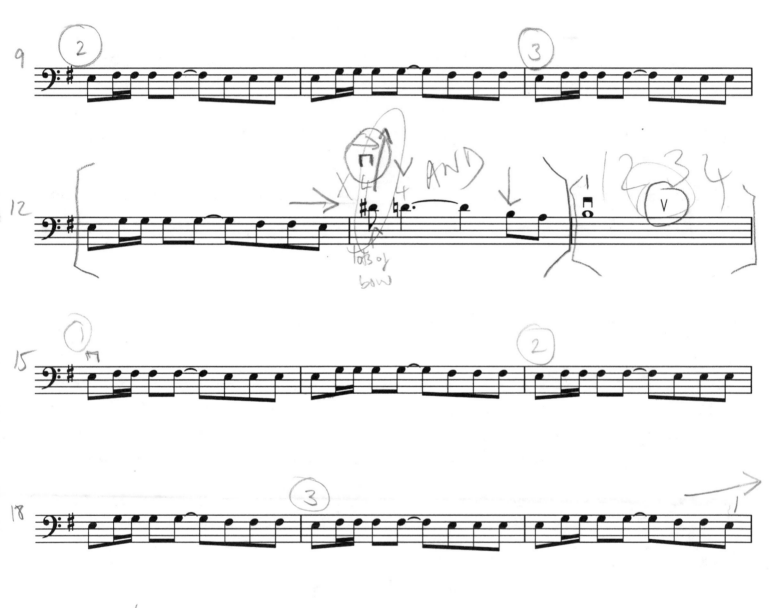

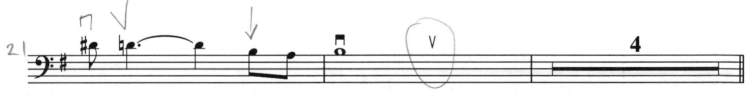

With a slight swing feeling

THUNDERBALL

Lyric by DON BLACK
Music by JOHN BARRY

IFM0403CD

TOMORROW NEVER DIES

Words and Music by
SHERYL CROW and
MITCHELL FROOM

THE WORLD IS NOT ENOUGH

Lyrics by DON BLACK
Music by DAVID ARNOLD

NOBODY DOES IT BETTER
(From "The Spy Who Loved Me")

Lyrics by CAROLE BAYER SAGER
Music by MARVIN HAMLISCH

IFM0403CD

LIVE AND LET DIE

Words and Music by
PAUL McCARTNEY and
LINDA McCARTNEY

YOU ONLY LIVE TWICE

Lyric by LESLIE BRICUSSE
Music by JOHN BARRY

IFM0403CD

Unlock the Magic of Popular Music for Strings!

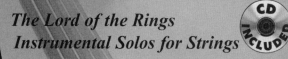

The Lord of the Rings
Instrumental Solos for Strings

This edition offers 12 major themes from the blockbuster trilogy and includes the piano accompaniment and CD. From *The Fellowship of the Ring*: The Prophecy • In Dreams • Concerning Hobbits • Many Meetings • The Black Rider. From *The Two Towers*: Gollum's Song • Rohan • Evenstar • Forth Eorlingas. From *The Return of the King*: Into the West • The Steward of Gondor • Minas Tirith. Available for violin (IFM0412CD), viola (IFM0413CD), and cello (IFM0414CD).

Harry Potter and the Chamber of Secrets:
Selected Themes from the Motion Picture

All editions are compatible and can be played separately or together. The included CD contains a demonstration of each song followed by a play-along track. *Titles are:* The Chamber of Secrets • Dobby the House Elf • Family Portrait • Fawkes the Phoenix • Gilderoy Lockhart • Harry's Wondrous World • Hedwig's Theme • Moaning Myrtle • Nimbus 2000. Available for violin (IFM0247CD), viola (IFM0248CD), and cello (IFM0249CD).

Paul Revere Award Winner

Movie Instrumental Solos
for Strings

Available with an accompaniment CD, including a demo track and a play-along track. *Titles are:* In Dreams (from *The Lord of the Rings: The Fellowship of the Ring*) • Across the Stars (from *Star Wars*®: Episode II *Attack of the Clones*) • Duel of the Fates (from *Star Wars*®: Episode I *The Phantom Menace*) • Fawkes the Phoenix (from *Harry Potter and the Chamber of Secrets*) • Gollum's Song (from *The Lord of the Rings: The Two Towers*) • James Bond Theme (from *Die Another Day*) • Goldfinger (from *Goldfinger*) • Hedwig's Theme (from *Harry Potter and the Sorcerer's Stone*) • October Sky (from *October Sky*) • Theme from *Jurassic Park*. Available for violin (IFM0315CD), viola (IFM0316CD), and cello (IFM0317CD).

The James Bond Collection
for Strings

All of the excitement of James Bond is now in an incredible collection for strings. *The James Bond Collection for Strings* features favorite James Bond movie themes with an accompaniment CD. *Titles include:* Diamonds Are Forever • For Your Eyes Only • From Russia with Love • Goldfinger • The James Bond Theme • Live and Let Die • Nobody Does It Better • On Her Majesty's Secret Service • Thunderball • Tomorrow Never Dies • The World Is Not Enough • You Only Live Twice. Available for violin (IFM0401CD), viola (IFM0402CD), and cello (IFM0403CD).

AD1172 9/04

TOMORROW NEVER DIES

Words and Music by
SHERYL CROW and
MITCHELL FROOM

Tomorrow Never Dies - 6 - 1
IFM0403CD

Tomorrow Never Dies - 6 - 2
IFM0403CD

30

Tomorrow Never Dies - 6 - 3
IFM0403CD

Tomorrow Never Dies - 6 - 6
IFM0403CD

THE WORLD IS NOT ENOUGH

Lyrics by DON BLACK
Music by DAVID ARNOLD

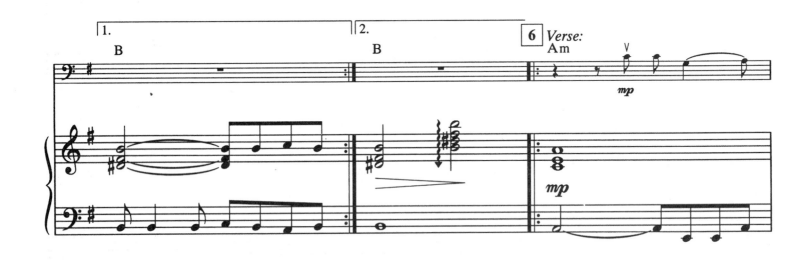

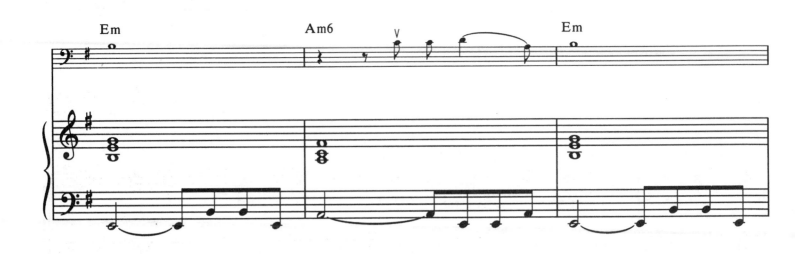

The World Is Not Enough - 4 - 1
IFM0403CD

NOBODY DOES IT BETTER

(From "The Spy Who Loved Me")

Lyrics by CAROLE BAYER SAGER
Music by MARVIN HAMLISCH

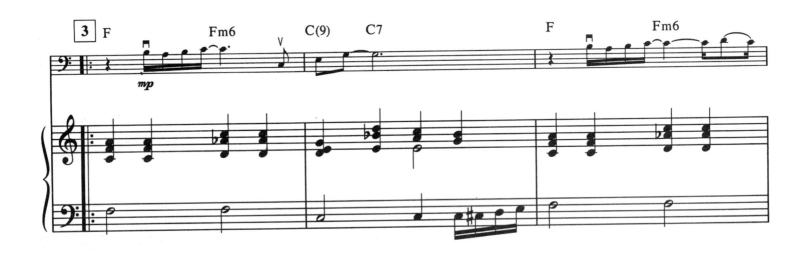

Nobody Does It Better - 3 - 1
IFM0403CD

LIVE AND LET DIE

Words and Music by
PAUL McCARTNEY and
LINDA McCARTNEY

Live and Let Die - 5 - 1
IFM0403CD

Live and Let Die - 5 - 3
IFM0403CD

44

Live and Let Die - 5 - 4
IFM0403CD

YOU ONLY LIVE TWICE

Lyric by LESLIE BRICUSSE
Music by JOHN BARRY

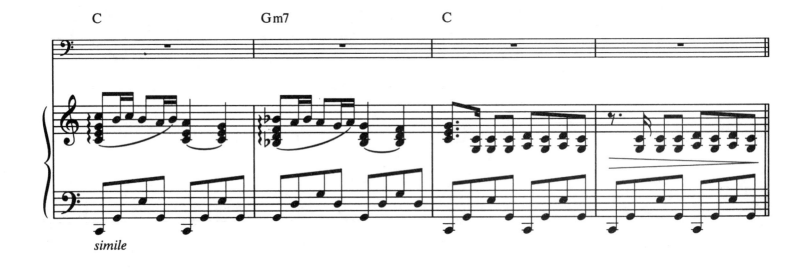

You Only Live Twice - 3 - 1
IFM0403CD